Jazzy Explores
The Library

by Sonja McGiboney

Copyright February 15, 2019
ISBN: 978-0 9600125-6-5

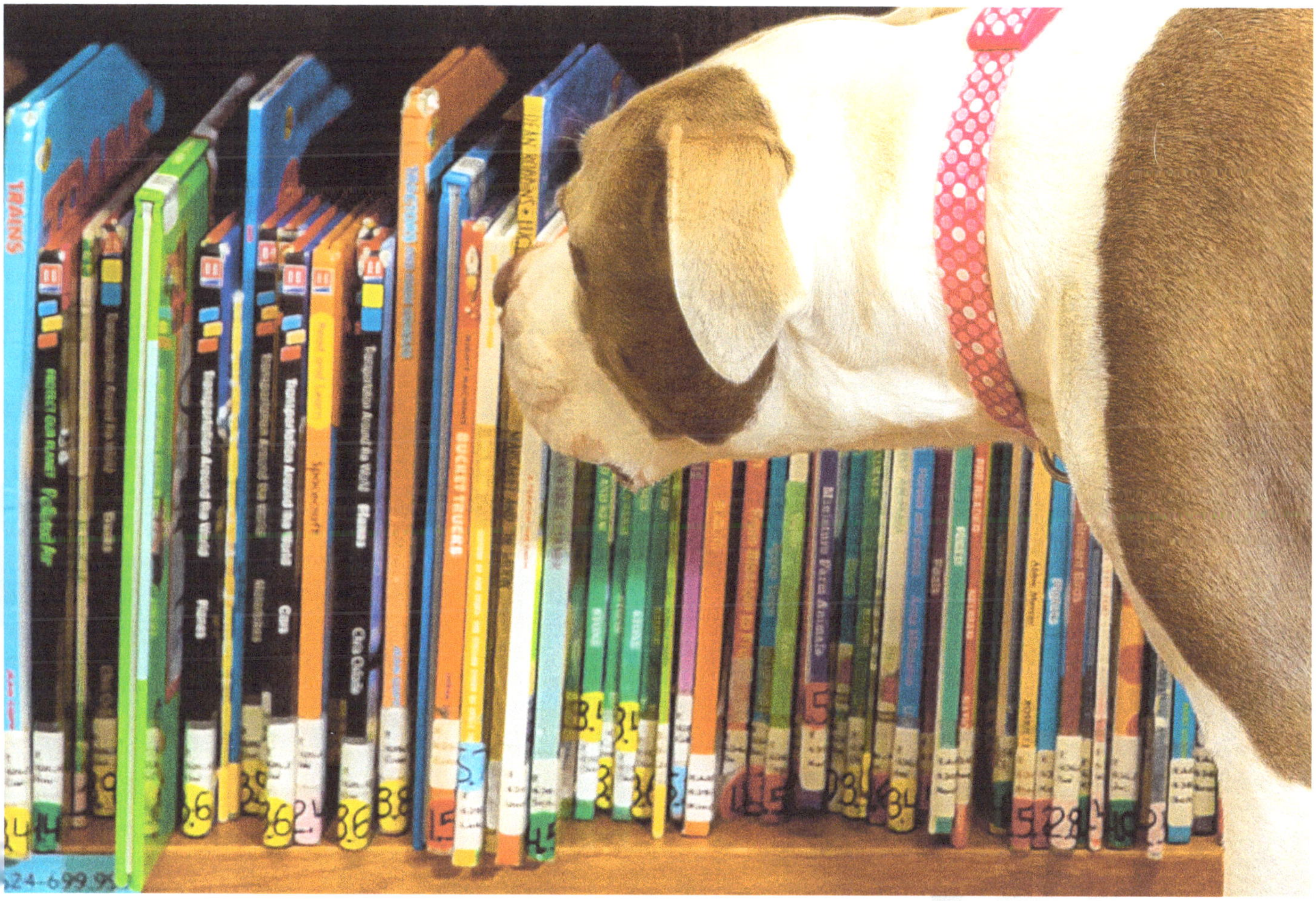

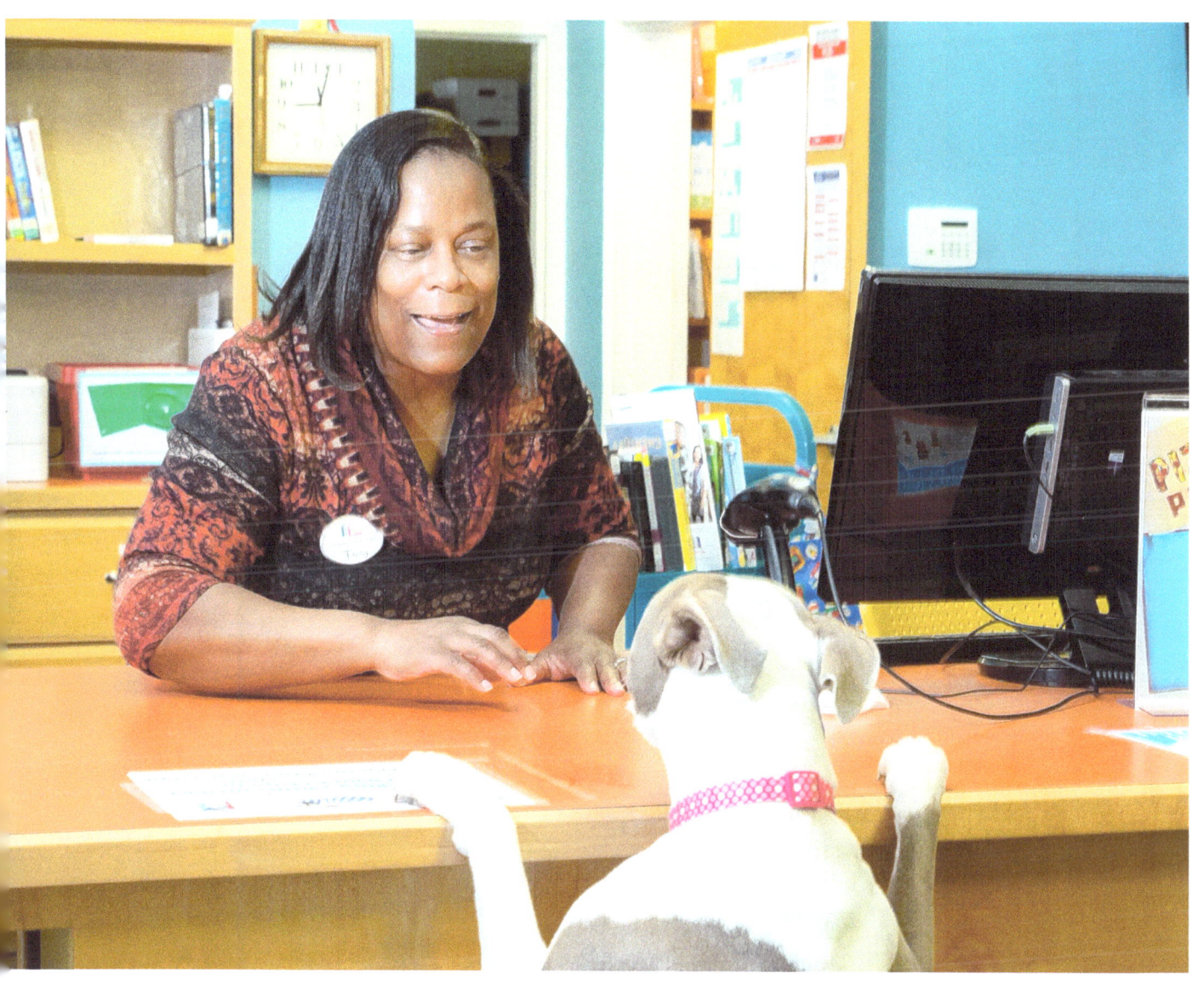

Jazzy heard there were bones in the library
And decided to take a look.
When she arrived, the librarian said,
"You will find them all in a book."

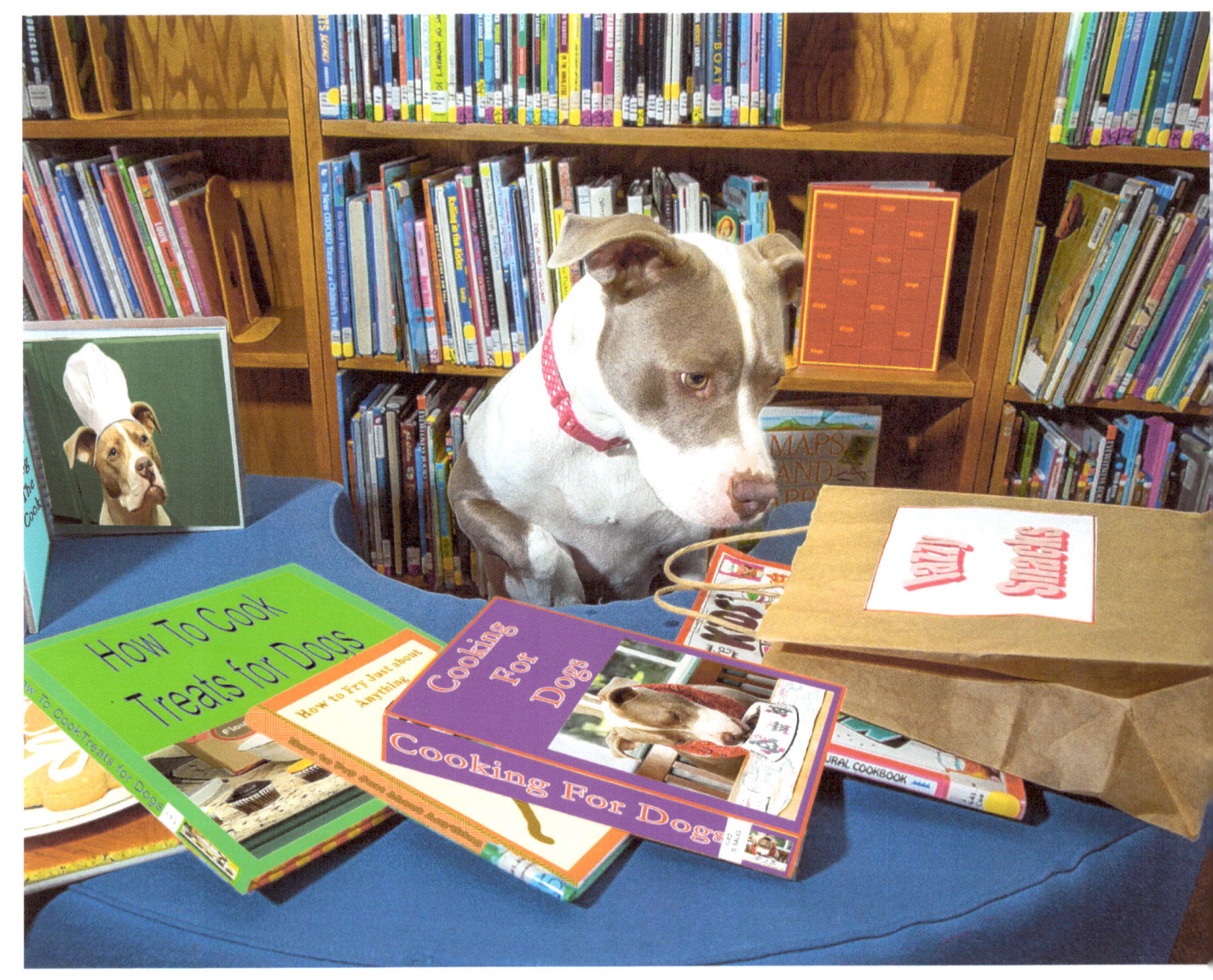

Jazzy set out to find the bones,
Sniffing away at each stack.
She found several books about making food
And suddenly needed a snack.

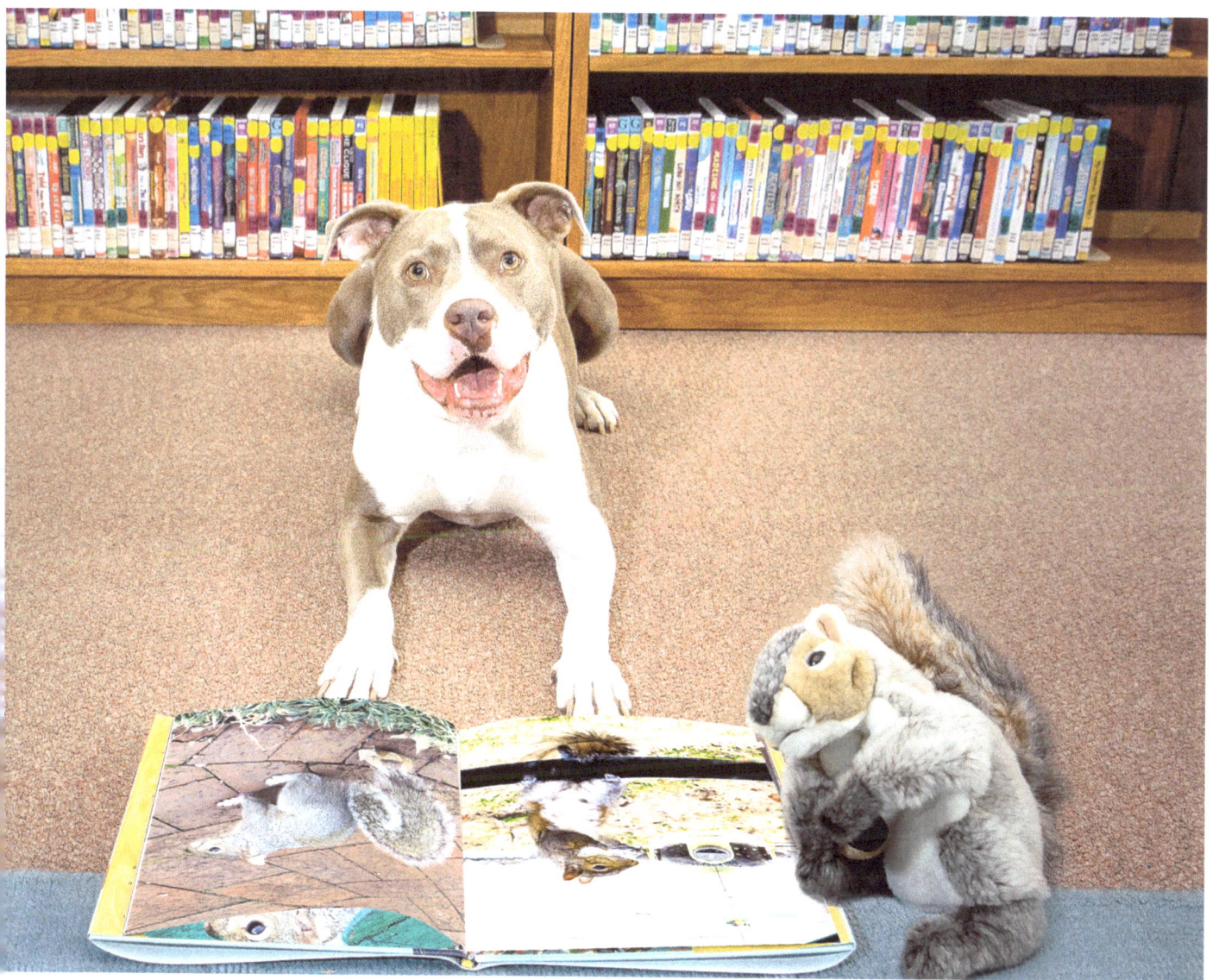

Near the food books were books about squirrels;
She couldn't help but look.
"How awesome!" Jazzy thought to herself.
"Squirrels that stay put in a book!"

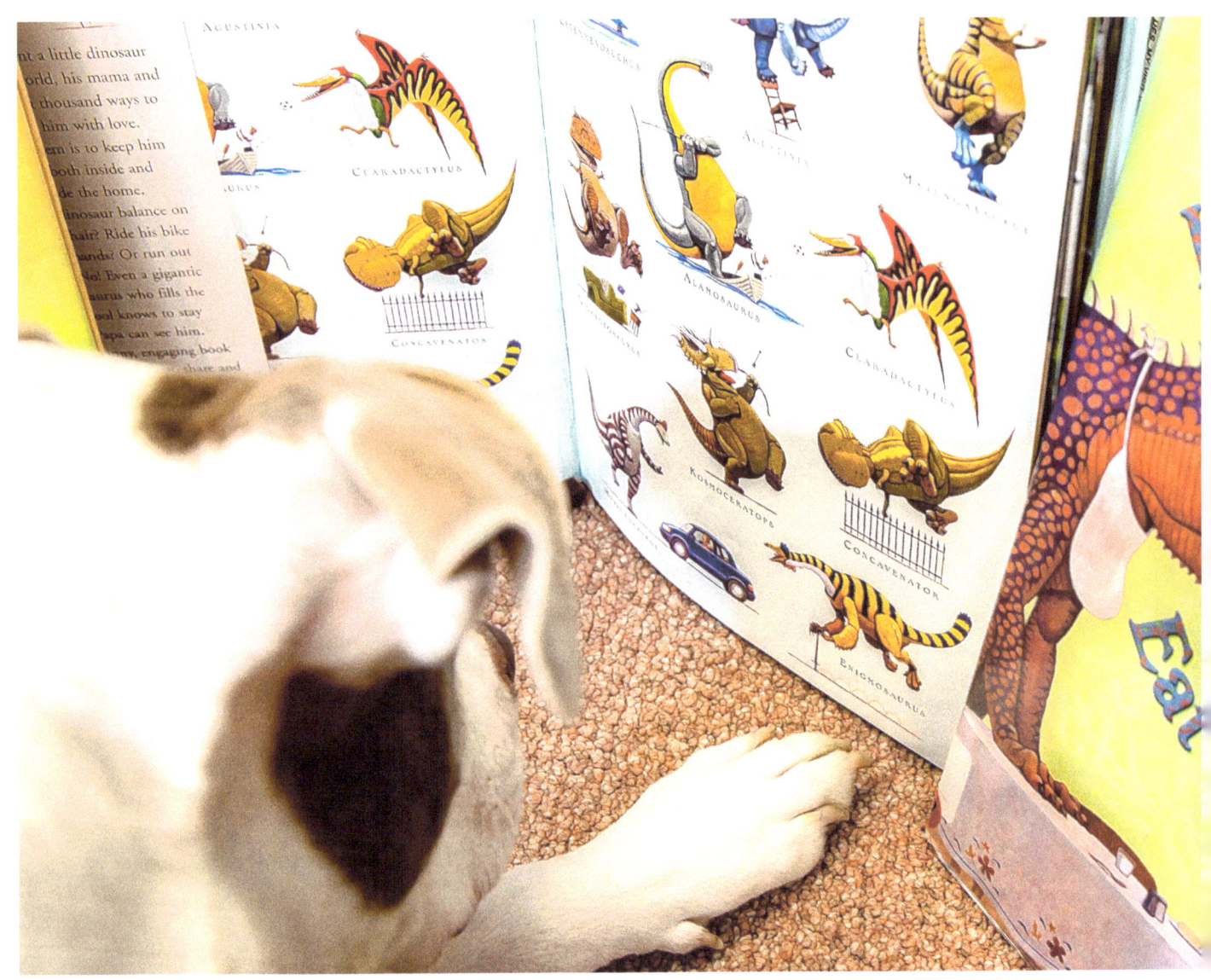

Tucked in a nook, away in the corner,
The dinosaurs waited to pounce.
Jazzy tried reading but finally gave up,
'Cause the names were too hard to pronounce.

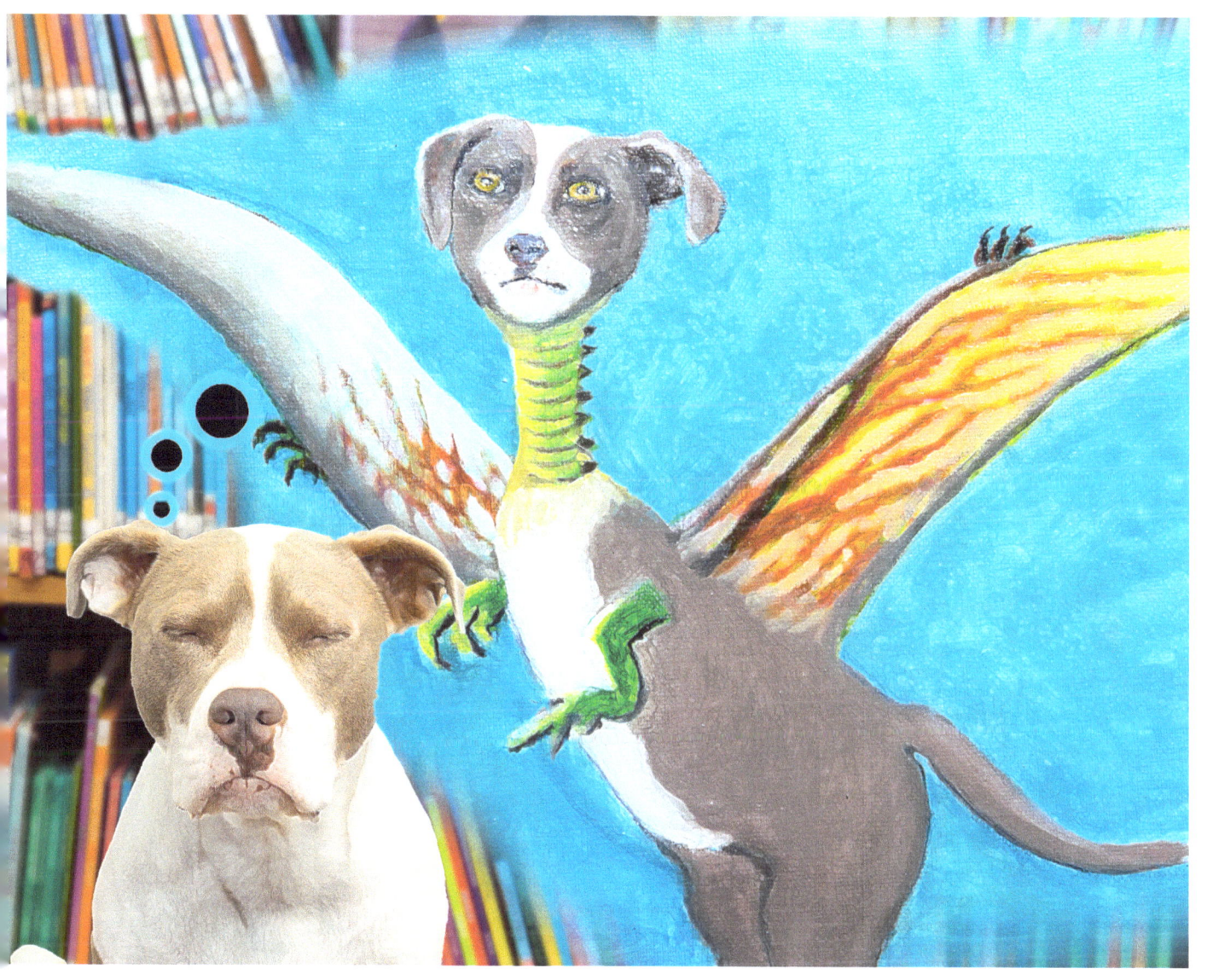

But she imagined herself having T-Rex hands
And long pterodactyl-like wings.
She imagined a neck like a diplodocus
And knew she could be anything!

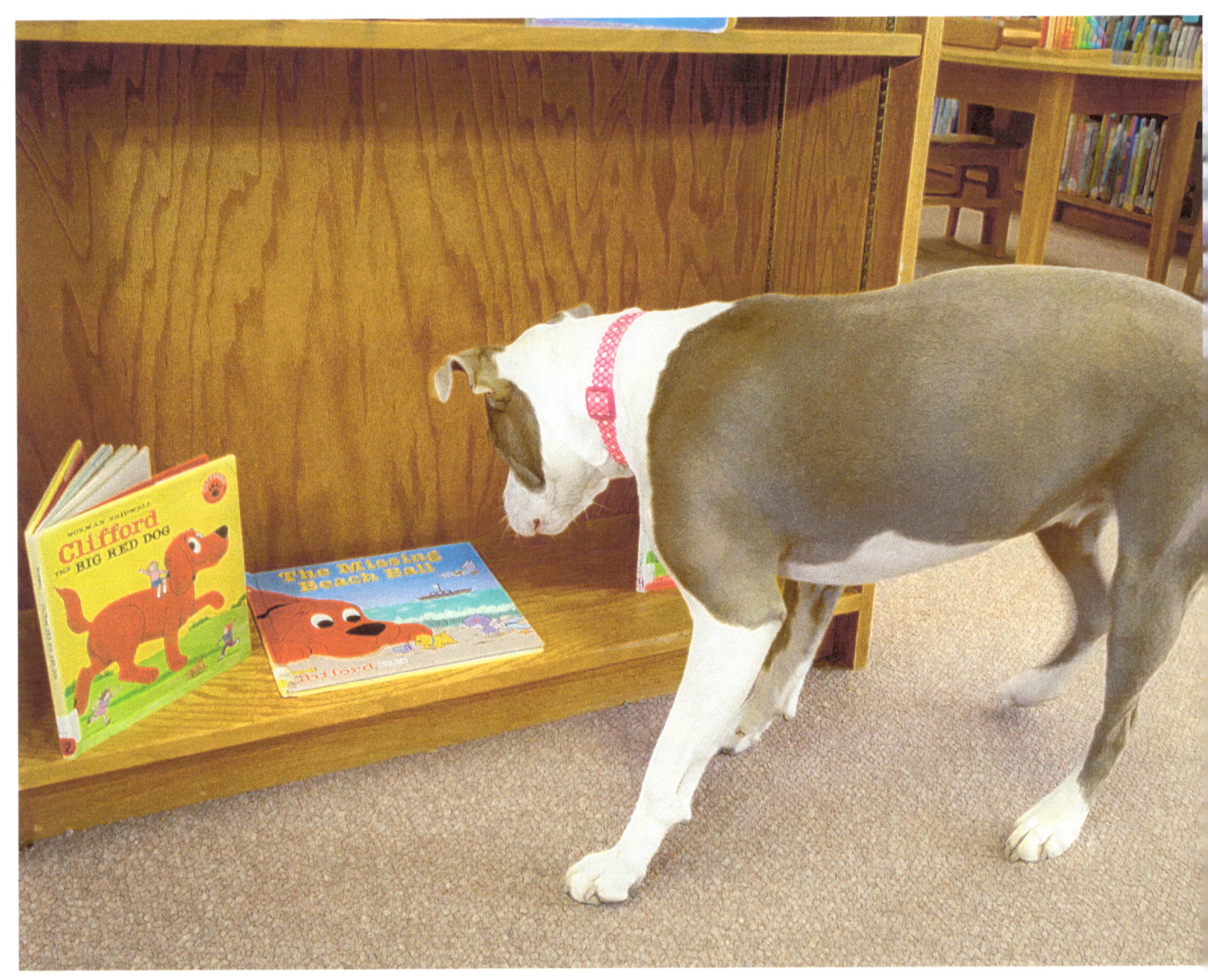

Jazzy continued to search for the bones,
Moving at full speed ahead.
She suddenly stopped and stared at a book:
A book with a dog that was red!

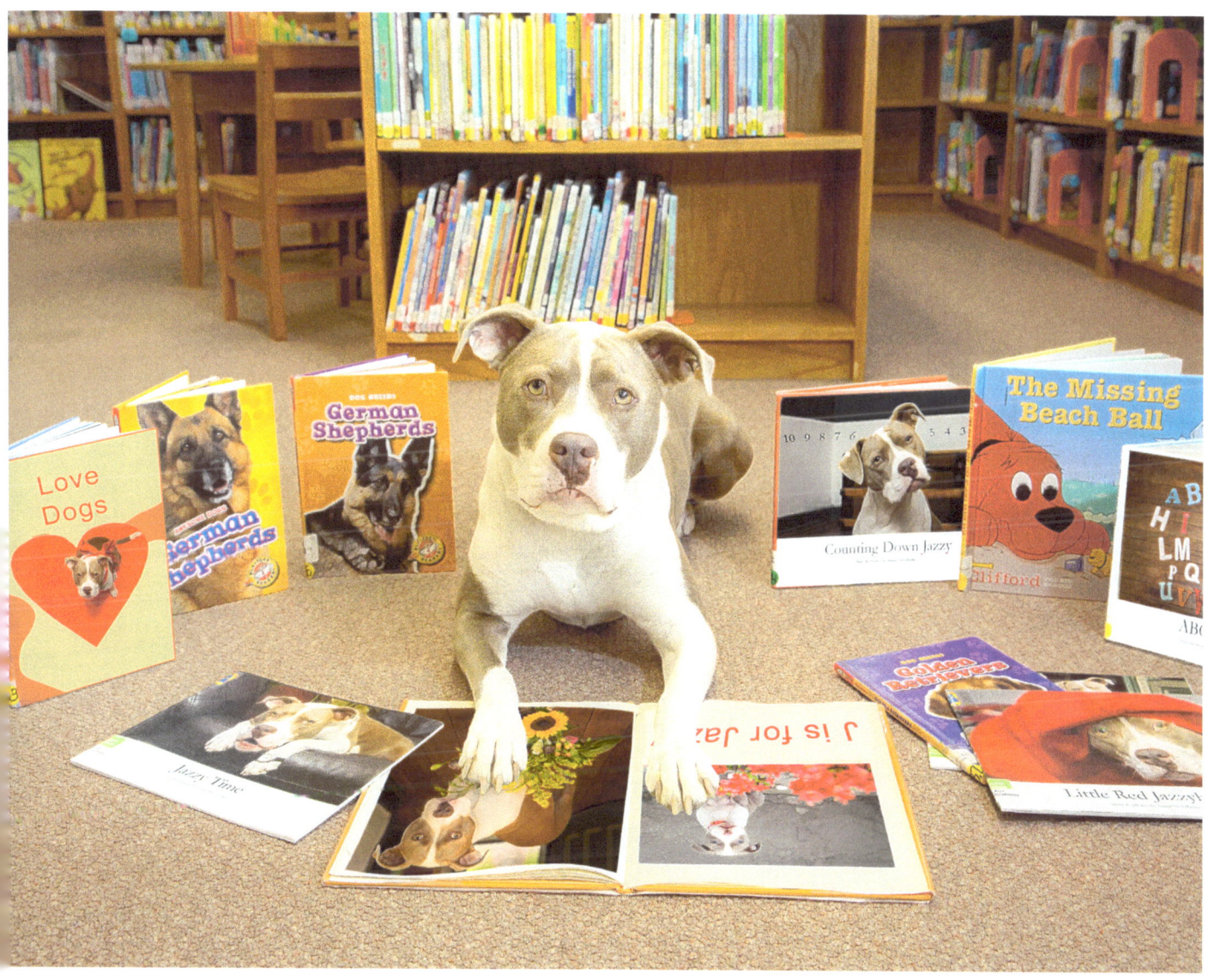

"What kind of dog book is that?" she asked,
Then searched for more on the shelf.
Happily she found dog books galore,
Including some of herself.

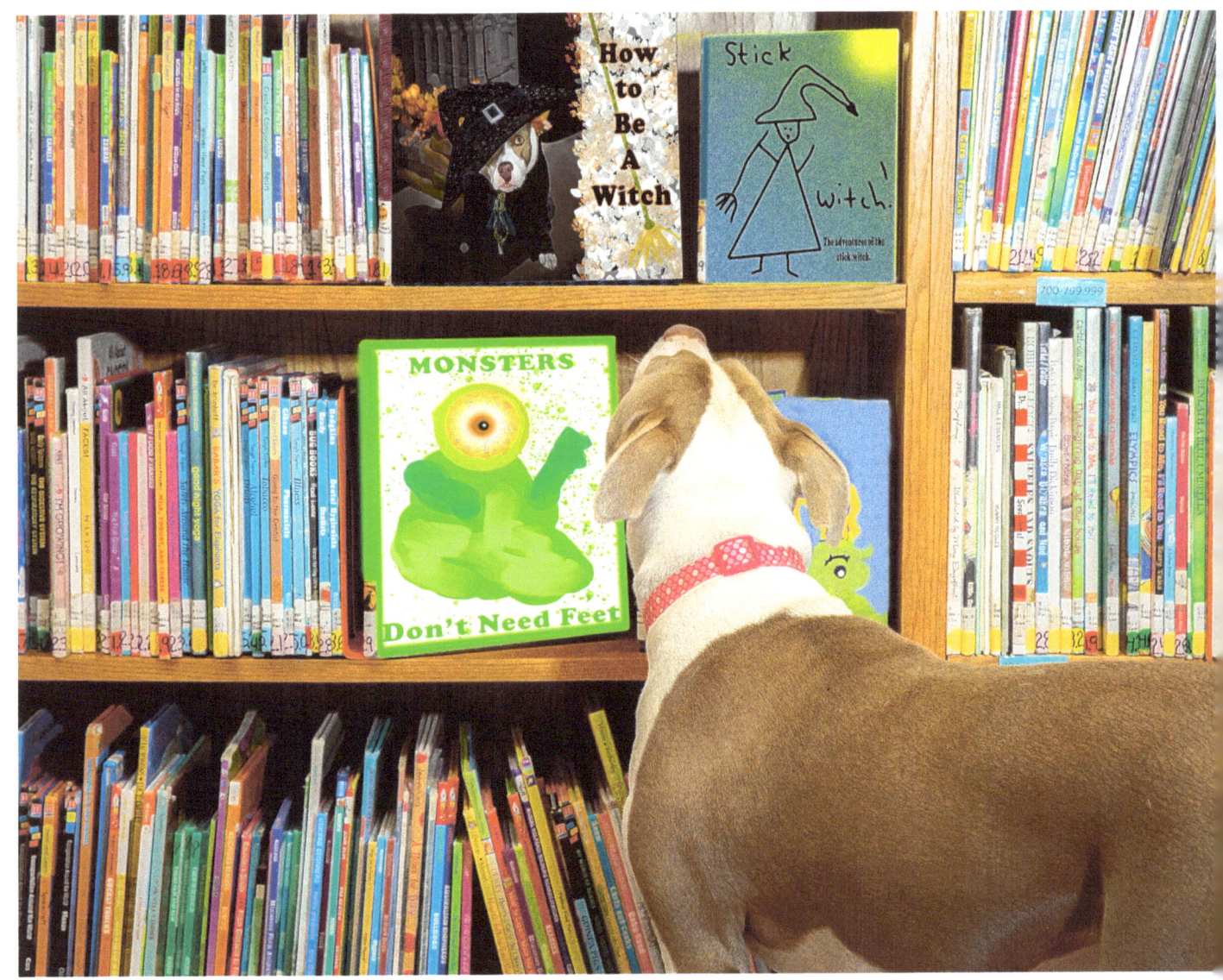

She continued to look, finding lots of neat books,
And having a lot of fun.
But then she saw books with witches and monsters
That made her want to RUN!

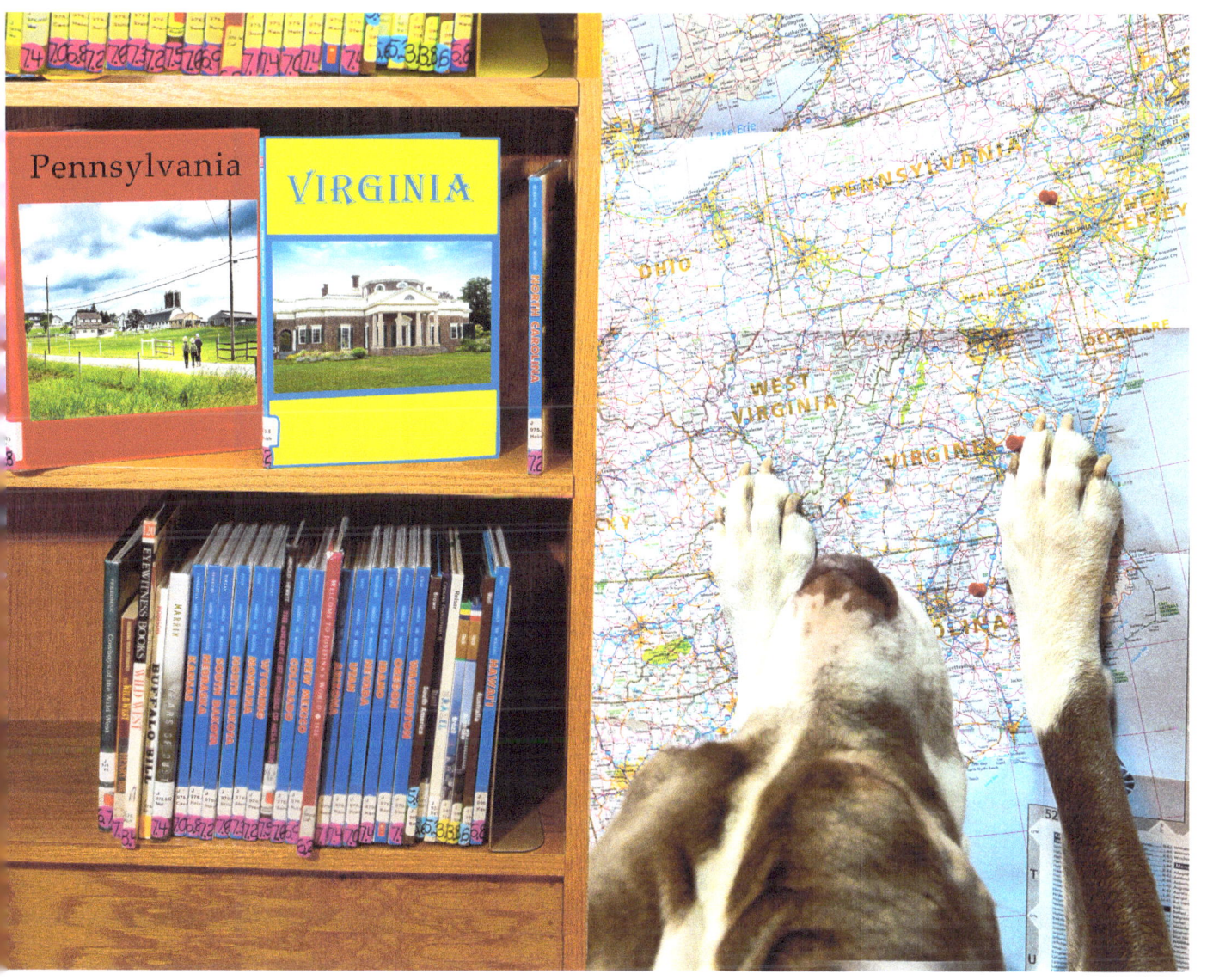

Jazzy passed books about her home
And thought of the places she'd been.
Pennsylvania, Virginia and North Carolina
She marked on a map with a pin.

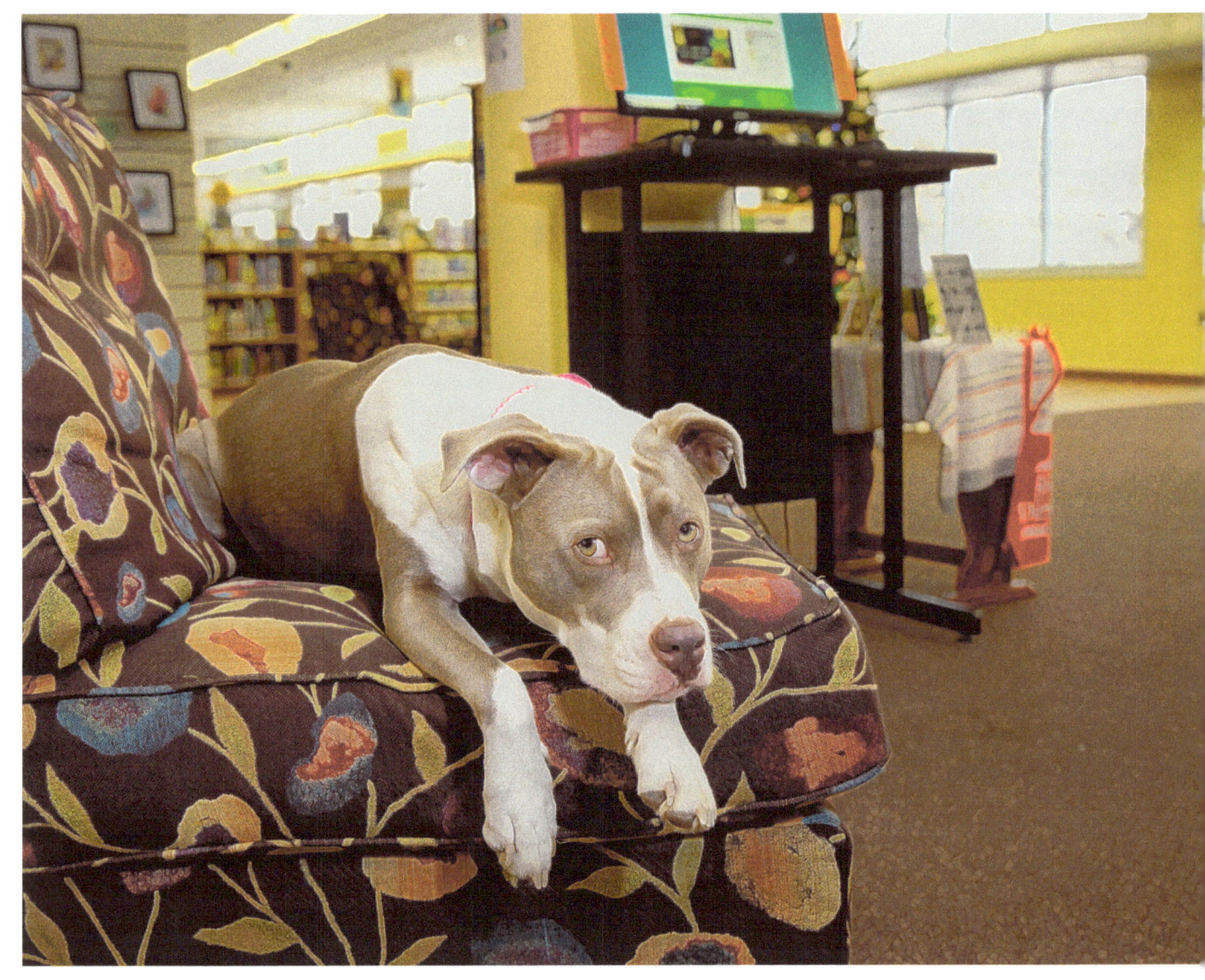

As fun as it was to read all the books,
She still hadn't found what she sought.
She jumped on the couch, made herself comfy
And gave it a lot of thought.

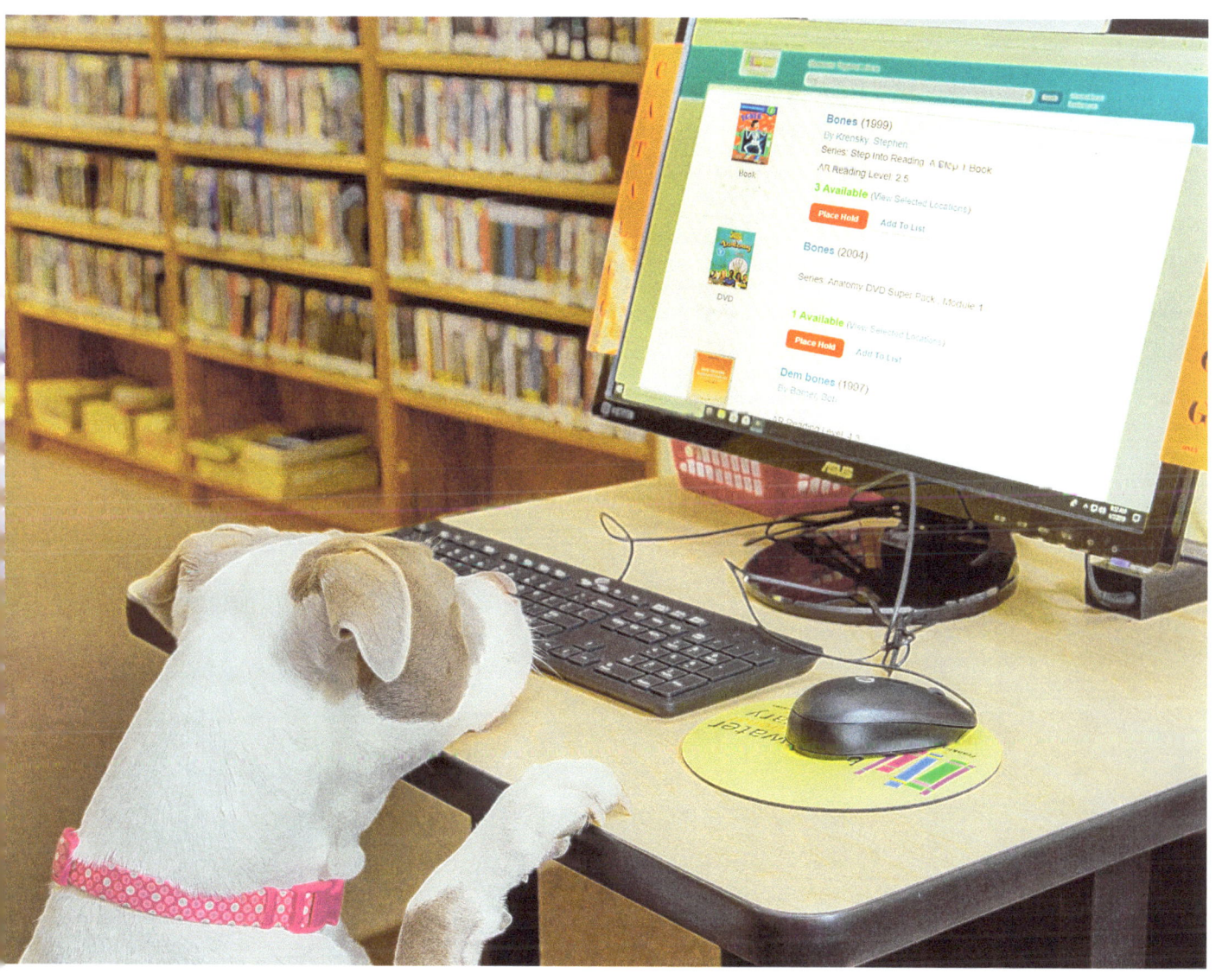

On the computer was a card catalog
Where Jazzy could look for direction.
And so it was, she found many bone books,
All in the science section.

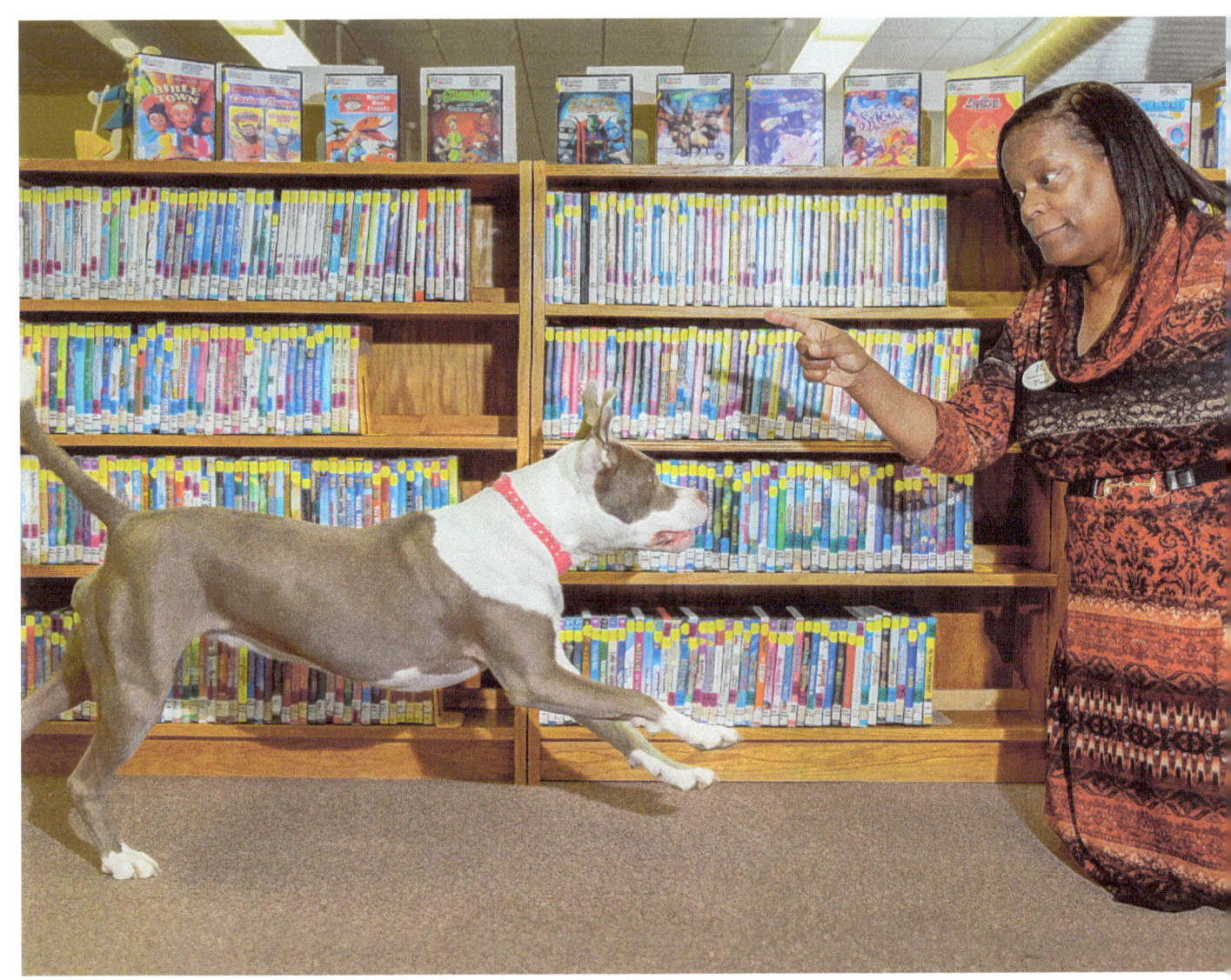

Excitedly, Jazzy ran towards the shelves,
Gaining a lot of speed.
The librarian stopped her and calmly said,
"No running, please!"

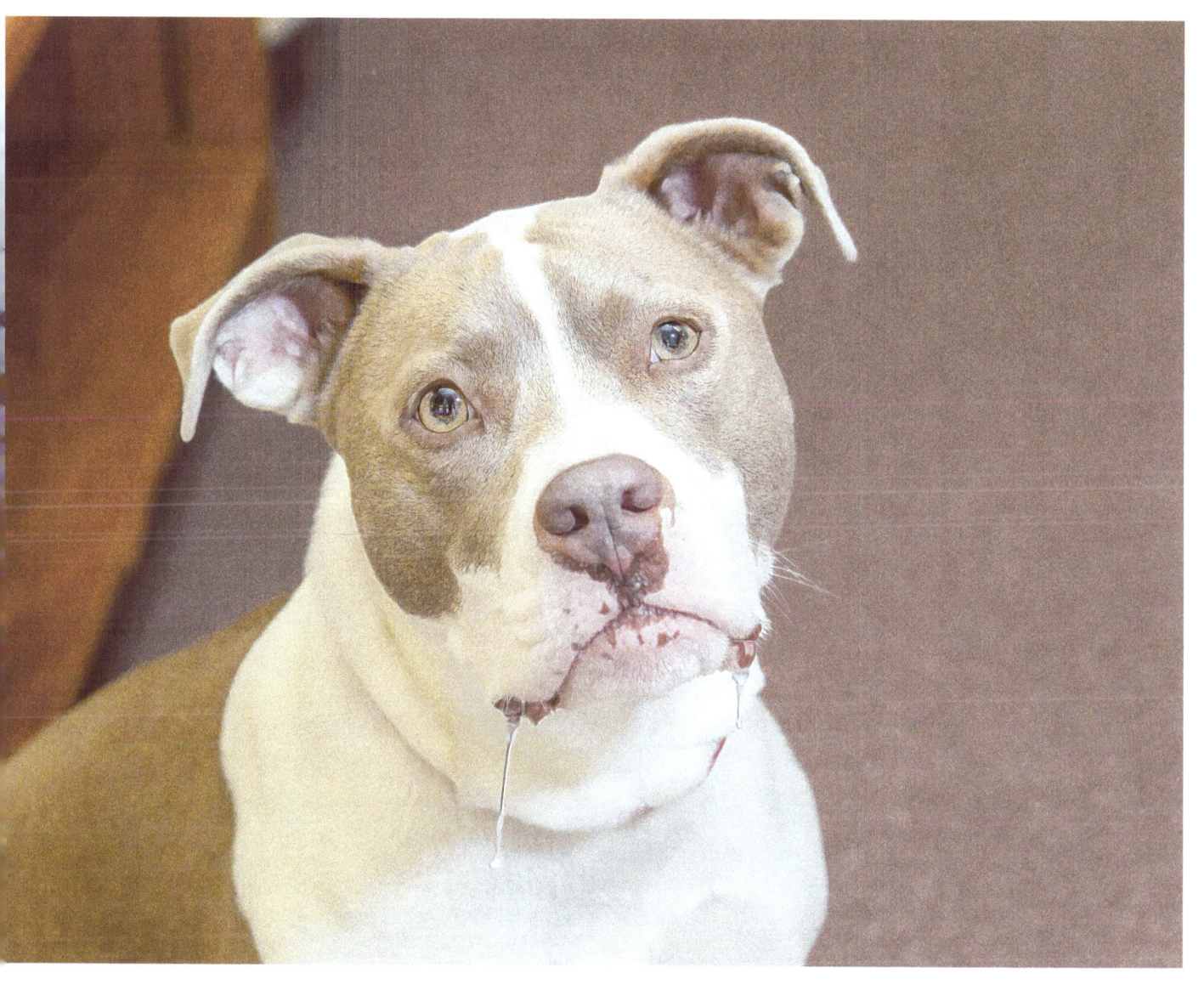

Jazzy walked the rest of the way,
Sorry that she broke a rule.
But when she found all the books about bones,
She couldn't help but drool.

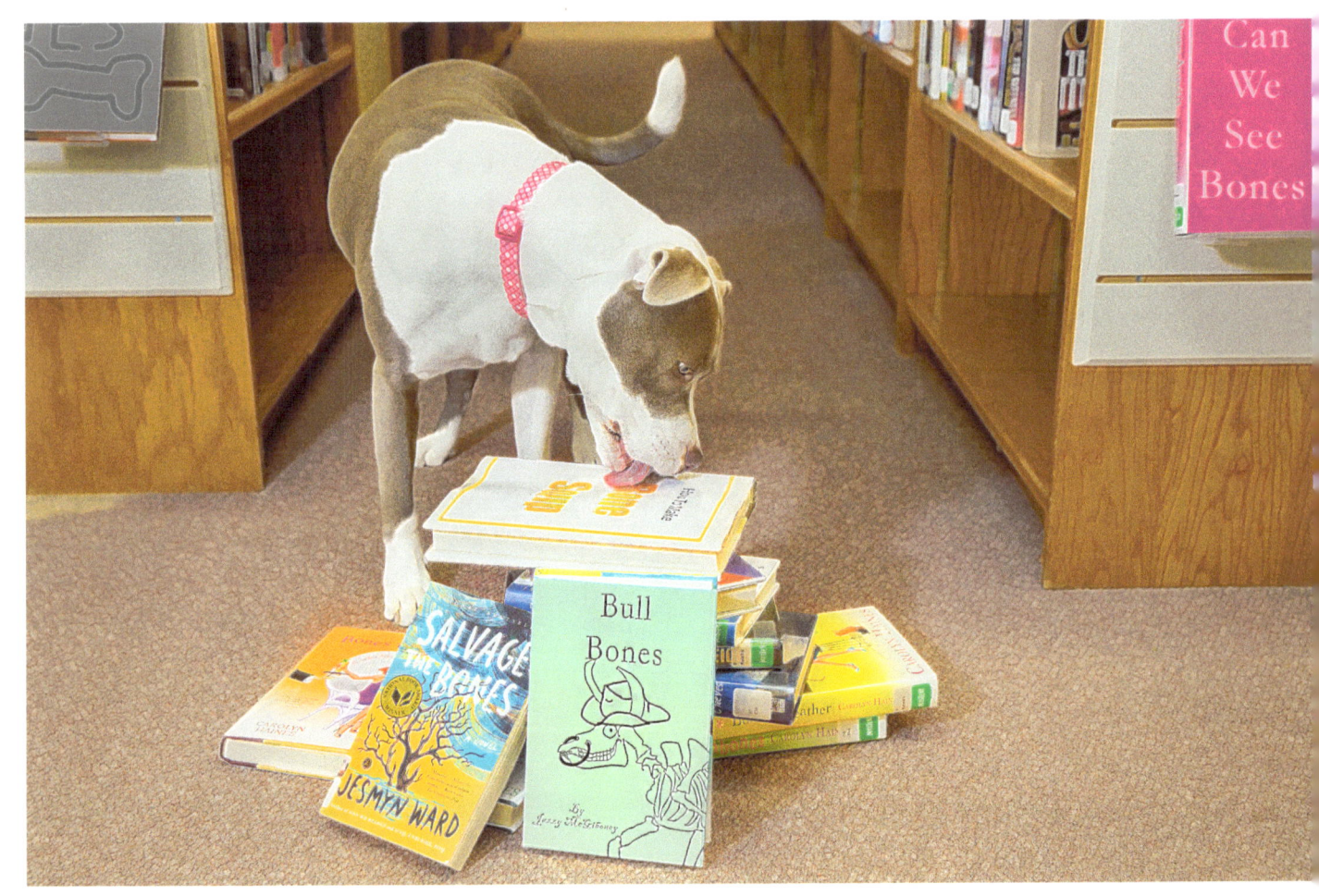

She gathered up books with bones on the covers;
The stack was getting quite thick.
When she had finished piling them all,
She gave the top one a lick.

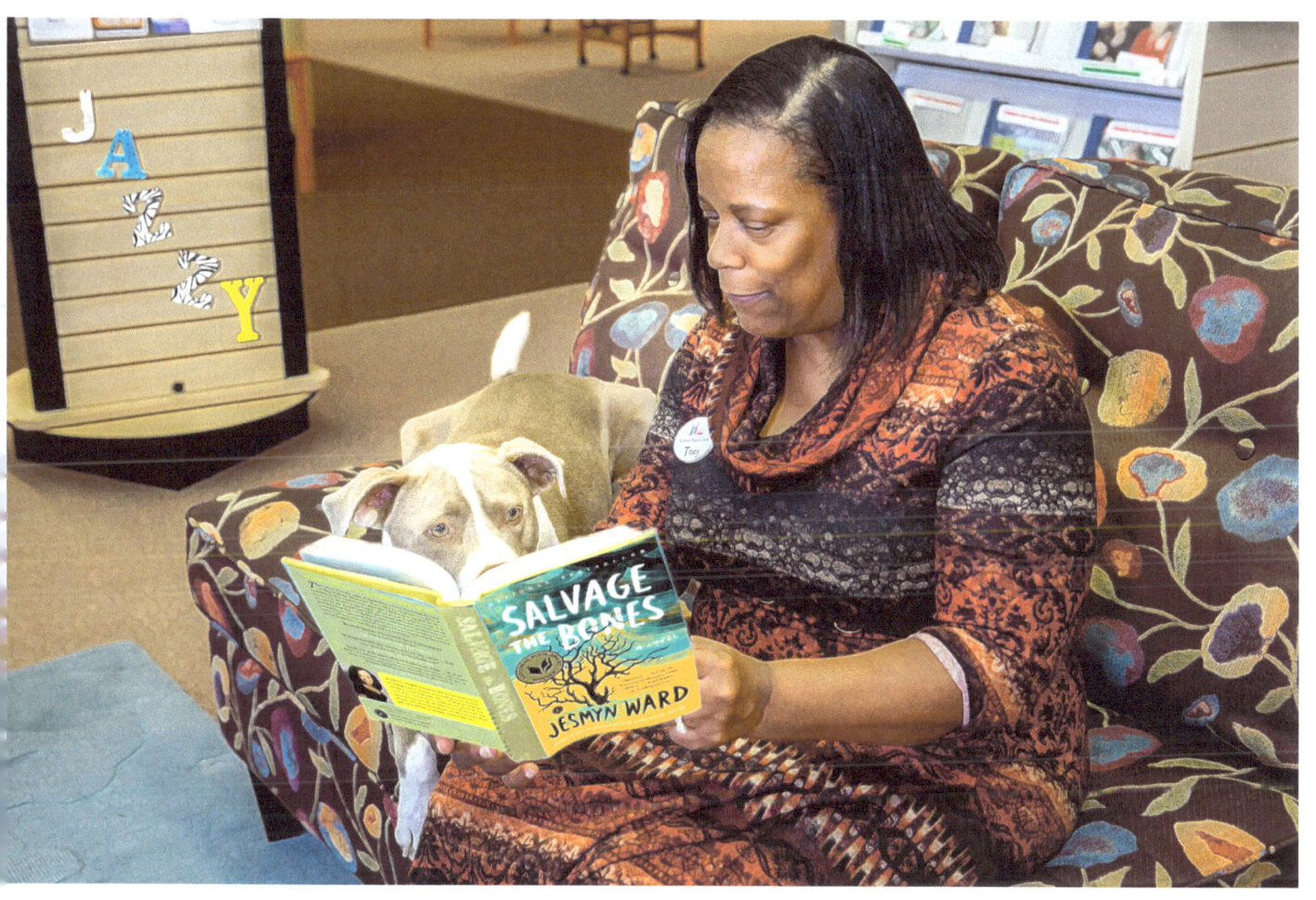

"Jazzy, I'm sorry!" the librarian said,
"I did not mean to mislead.
These books are not for you to eat;
They are here for you to read."

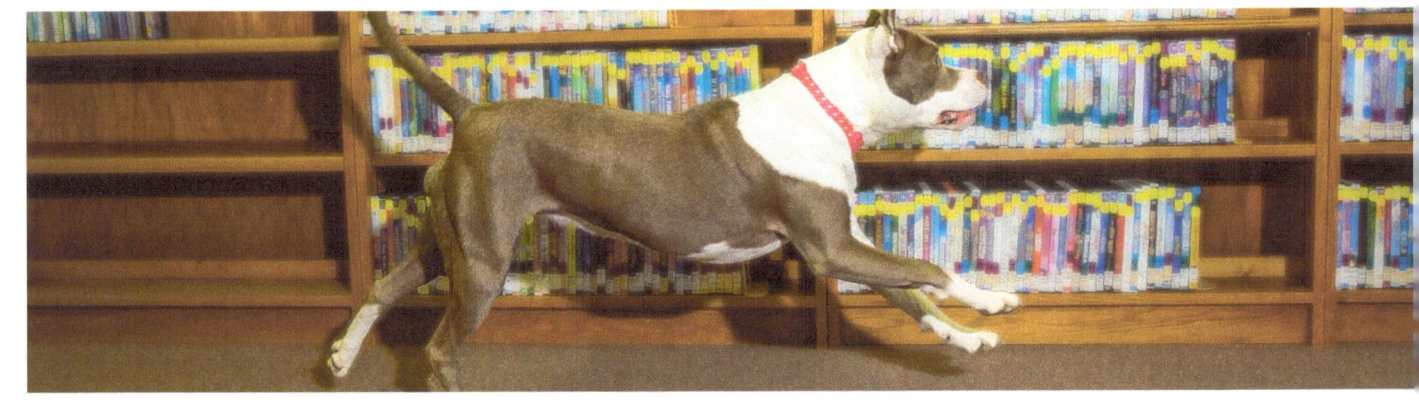

The Dewey Decimal System

When you found this book, it was in the fiction section. The book is a "made up" story. Librarians put fiction books away in alphabetical order, beginning with the first letter of the author's last name.

Non-fiction books, which are about things that are true, are put away differently.

In 1876, Melvil Dewey published a new way to organize books about real stuff. His way of organizing non-fiction books is still used today. The Dewey Decimal system gives books numbers based on what they are about. That makes it easier to find them on the shelves.

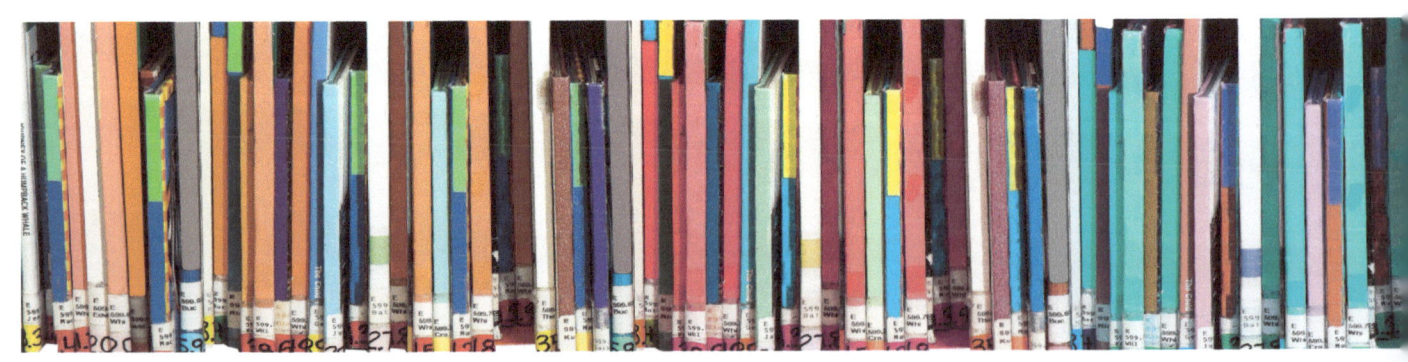

000 to 099

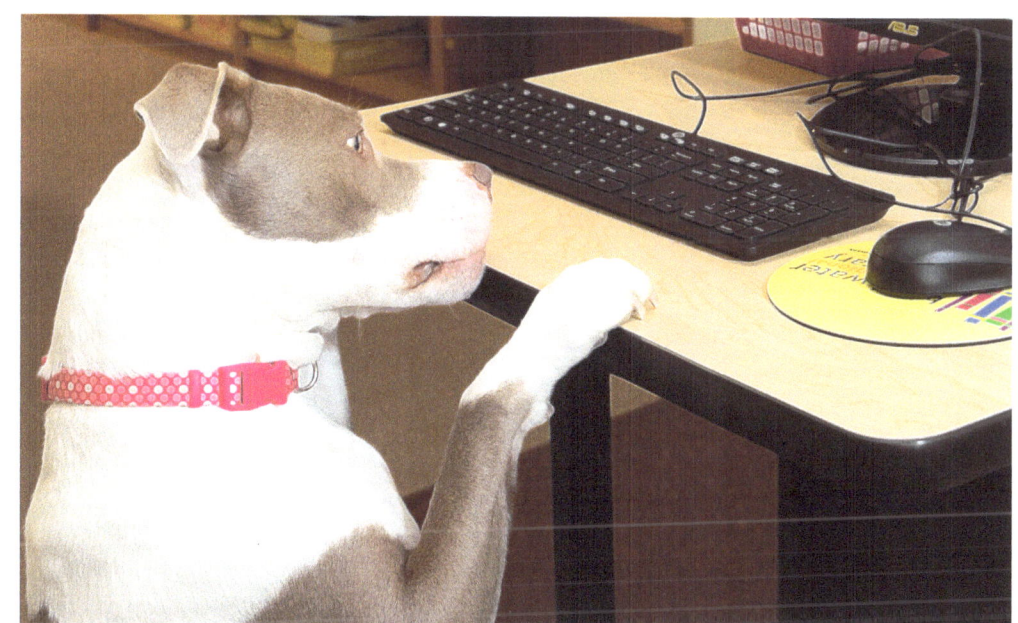

General Works * Computer Science * Information

Here you will find books that have a lot of information like in an encyclopedia or a journal.

100 to 199

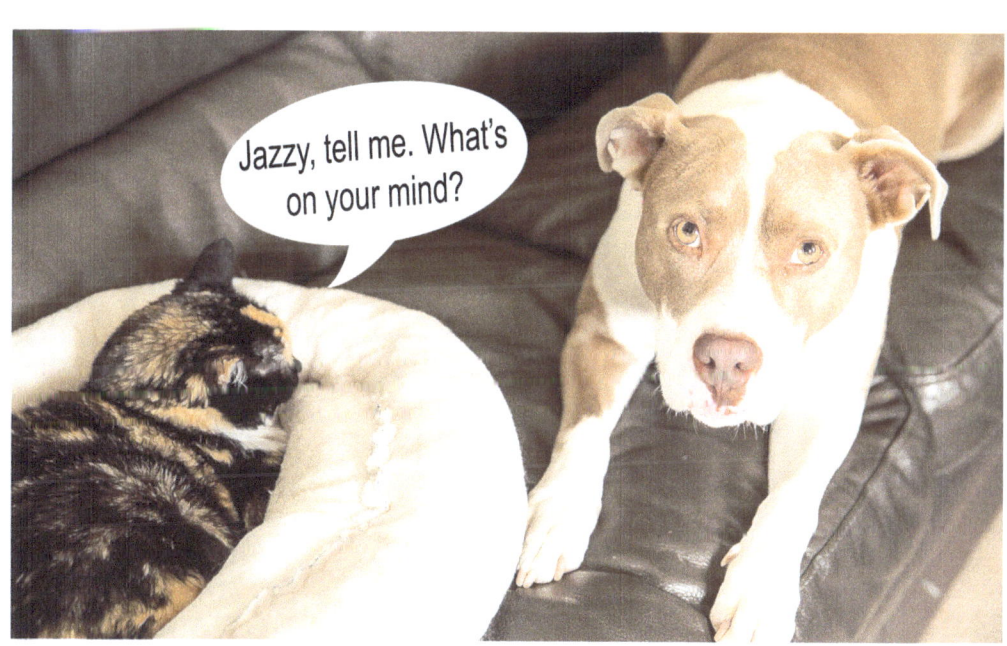

Philosophy * Psychology

Books in this section are about feelings and about how and why people think and act the way they do.

200
to
299

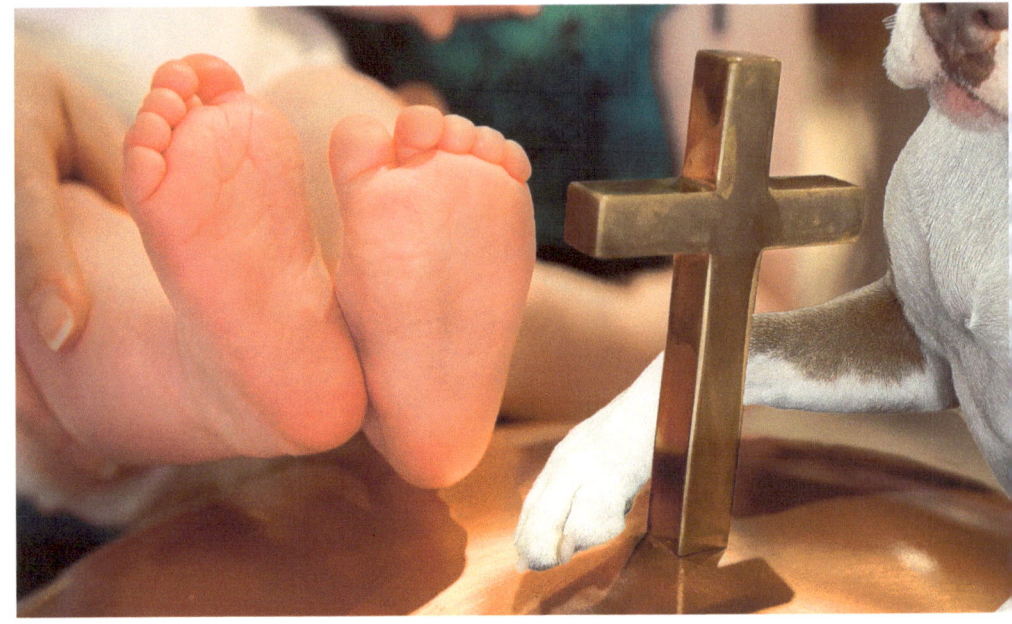

Religion

These books tell about the religions found all over the world and about the history of each religion.

300
to
399

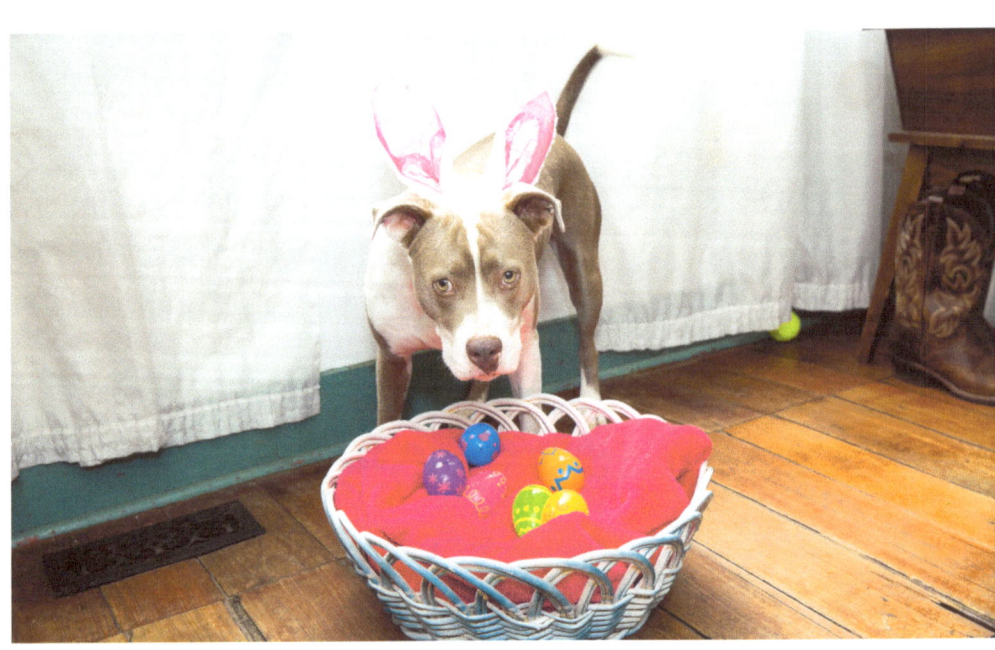

Social Sciences

Books here are about the rules humans use to get along, what their culture is like, and how they survive.

400
to
499

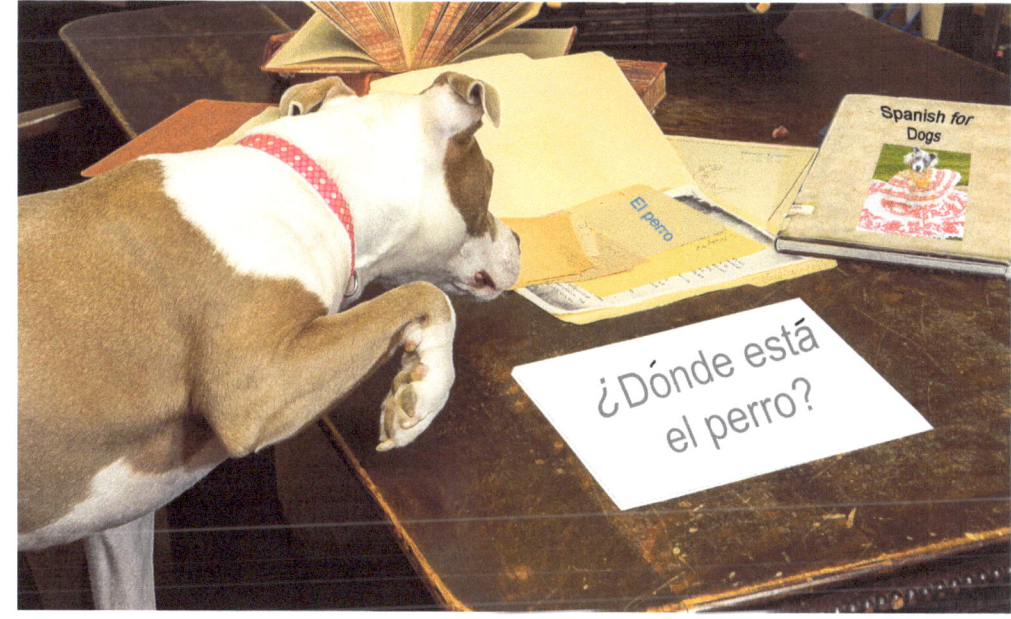

Language

This is where you go if you want to learn another language or get some help with English.

500
to
599

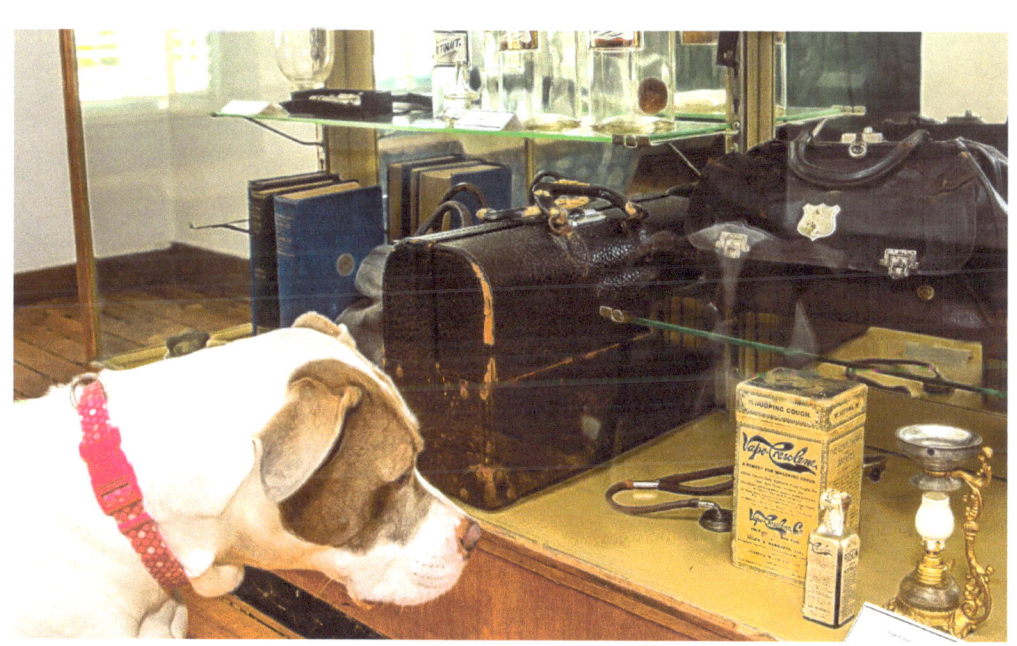

Science

Besides books about math, you can find books on chemistry, biology, astronomy, geography and many more earth sciences.

**600
to
699**

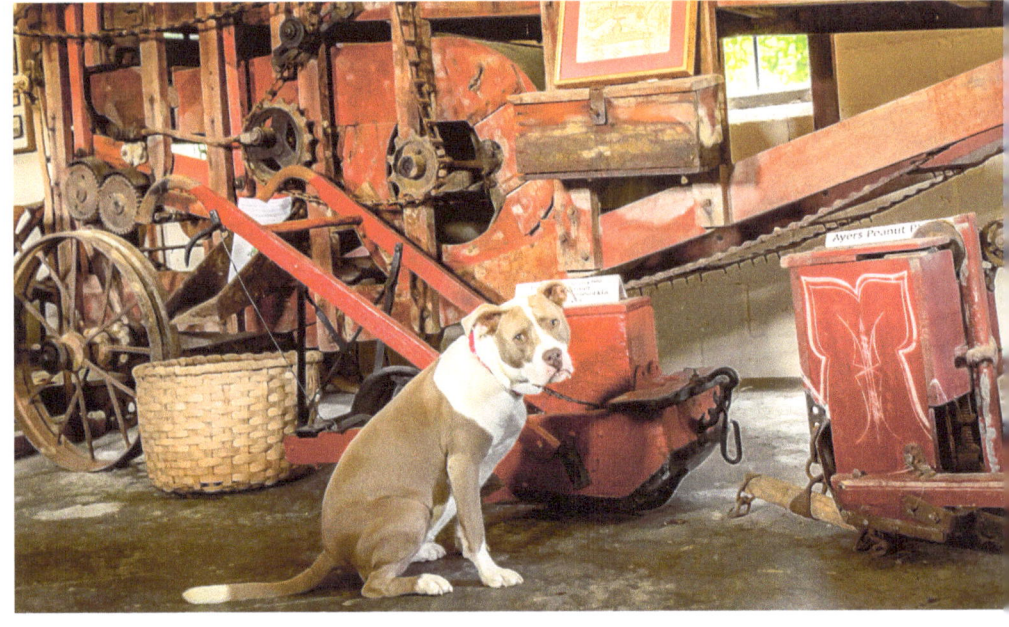

Technology * Applied Sciences

All kinds of topics on medicine, engineering, cooking, child rearing, management and construction are found here.

**700
to
799**

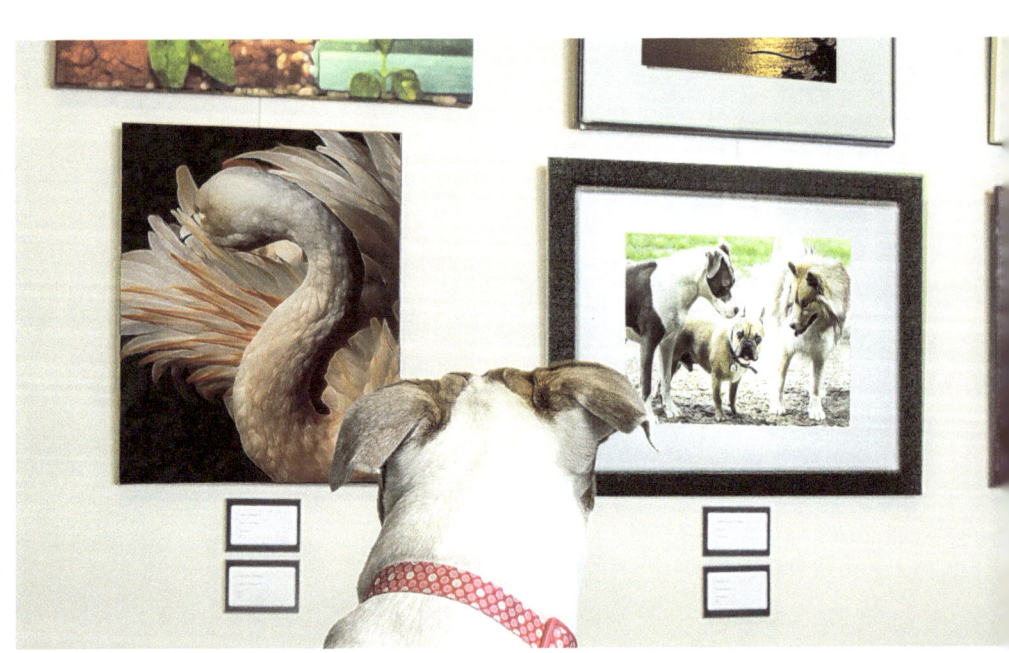

Arts * Recreation

This section has books on painting, sculpting, taking pictures, knitting, crafting, making music and musical instruments.

800
to
899

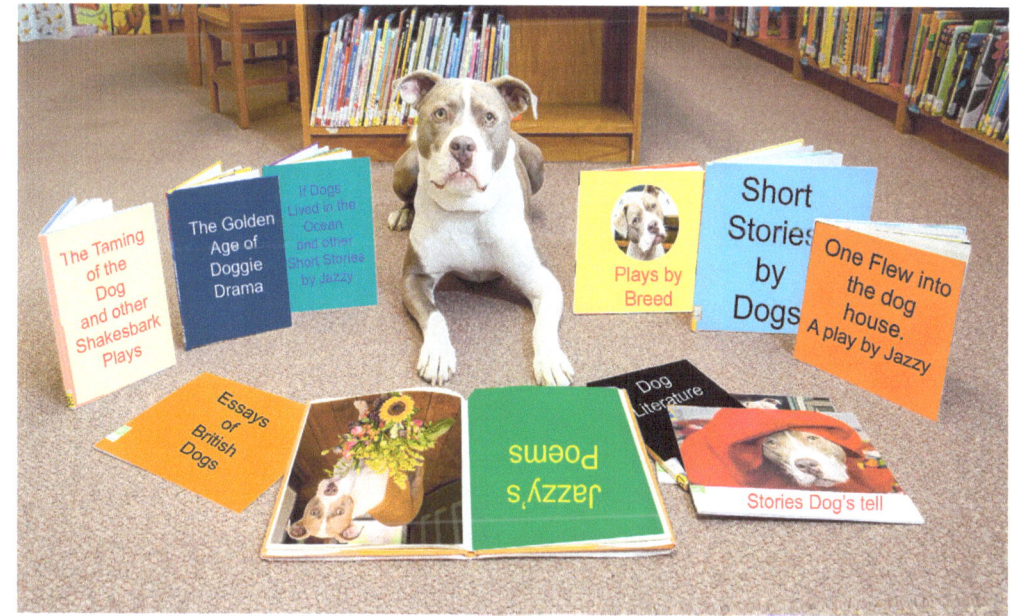

Literature

This is a large section of books that has poems, essays, stories from past cultures, plays, dramas, scripts and more.

900
to
999

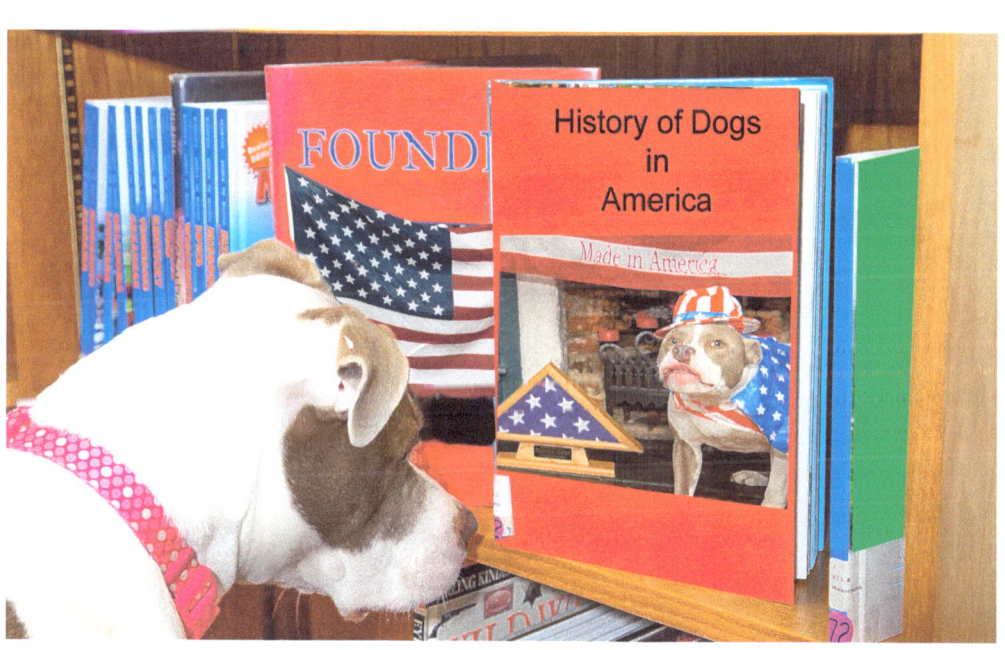

Geography * History * Travel

Books here can help you plan trips to wherever you want to go and tell the history of all those places.

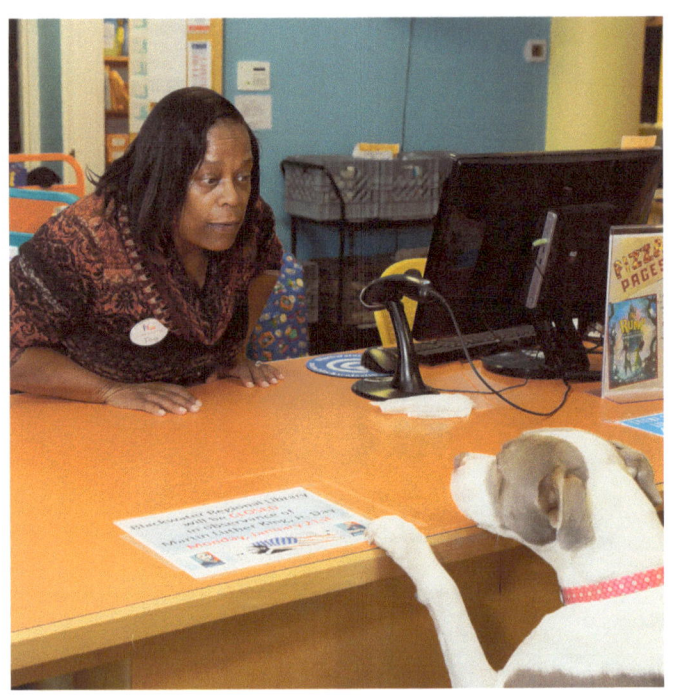

Tracy Frie was the librarian at the Blackwater Regional Library in Smithfield, Virginia.
She has since moved to New Mexico to be with her family.

Tracy loves reading and loves Jazzy.

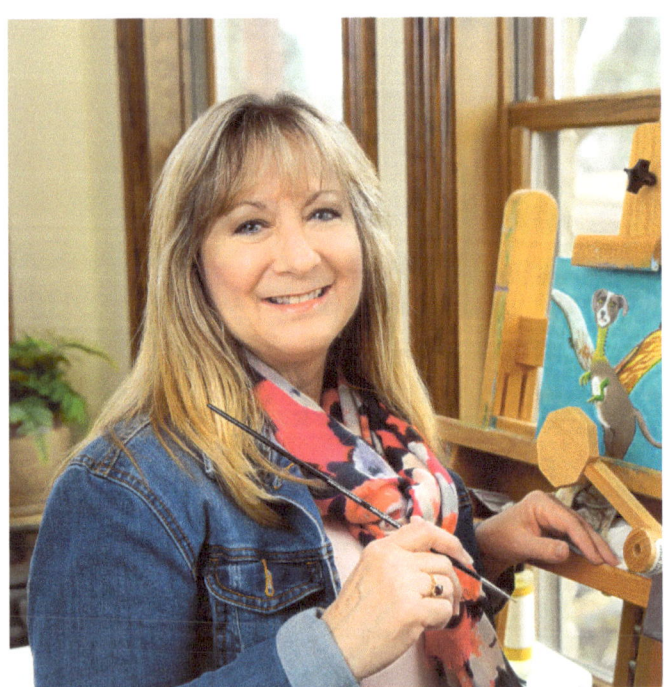

"Jazzy's Dream"
The picture of Jazzy's Dream was painted by Kim Abbott Holland.   Kim is a freelance painter in Smithfield, Virginia. You can find more of her work on Etsy at: ArtByKimberlyStudio

Email: khllnd@charter.net

Many thanks to the following publishers for allowing me to use portions of their books in my story.

Bellwether Media Inc: "German Shepherds" by Chris Bowman, 2016
Bellwether Media Inc: "German Shepherds" by Mari Schuh, 2009
Bellwether Media Inc: "Golden Retrievers" by Mari Schuh, 2009
Bloomsbury Publishing Plc: "Salvage the Bones" by Jesmyn Ward 2012
Deanna F Cook: Author of "The Kids' Multicultural Cookbook" 1995
Kensington Publishing Corp: "Bones to Pick" by Carolyn Haines, 2006
Scholastic Inc: "The Missing Beach Ball" by Norman Bridwell 2002
Scholastic Inc: "Clifford the Big Red Dog" by Norman Bridwell 2004
Scholastic Inc: "How Do Dinosaurs Stay Safe?" by Jane Yolen 2015
Scholastic Inc: "How Do Dinosaurs Eat Their Food?" by Jane Yolen 2005

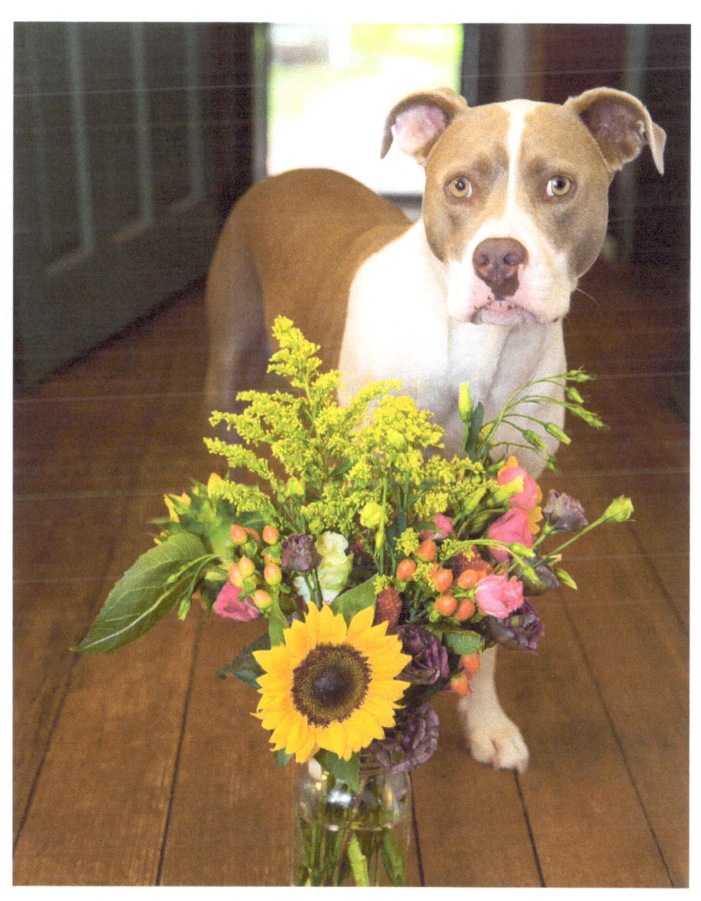

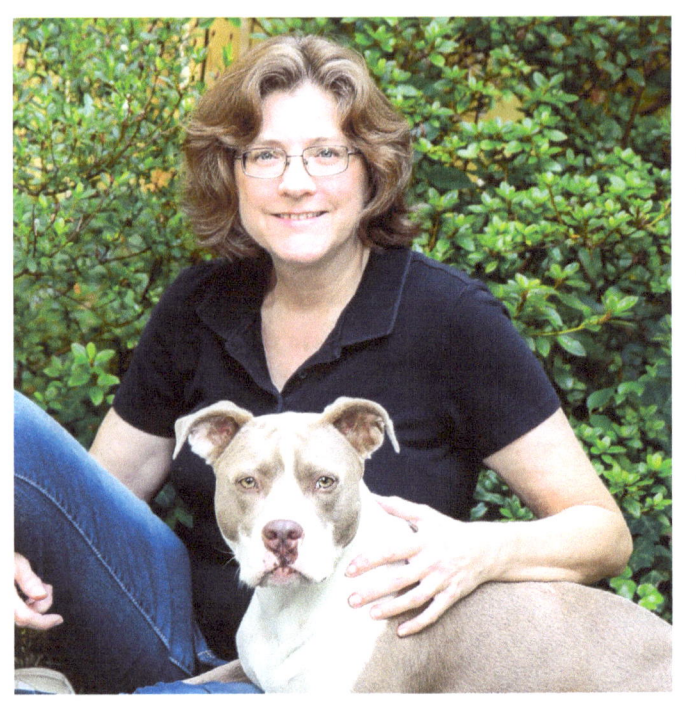

Sonja McGiboney grew up in Stowe, Pennsylvania. After obtaining her undergraduate degree in music from West Virginia University, she married Dale and accompanied him on his 25-year military career. She has two wonderful children, Rachel and Ryan, and now lives with Dale and Jazzy in Smithfield, Virginia. She loves taking photos and writing Jazzy's Books.

Check out all Jazzy's books!

1. ABC Jazzy
2. Counting Down Jazzy
3. Growing Up Jazzy
4. Hide and Seek - Jazzy's Alphabet Adventure
5. Jazzy and Friends
6. Jazzy Colors
7. Jazzy Time
8. Jazzy Shapes
9. Jazzy Explores the Library
10. Jazzy Explores Smithfield, VA
11. Jazzy Explores Murfreesboro, NC
12. Jazzy's Halloween - A Night in Ghouling Brook
13. Jazzy's Twelve Days of Christmas
14. Little Red Jazzyhood
15. Princess Jazzy - How to Prove You're a Princess